TO Denise.

The Light will
to see.
Your heart will
can feel
The Love that you have will always
be!

The Loss of a Child

My Story

Love and blessings

Jenny Ford

Jenny xxx

ISBN: 978-1-912243-97-6

Printed Edition
Also available in multiple e-book formats.

Published by
The Endless Bookcase Ltd
71 Castle Road, St Albans, Hertfordshire, AL1 5DQ
United Kingdom
www.theendlessbookcase.com

Cover image
Precious Memories Photography by Lottie

Illustrator
Lorena Lees

Editor
Matt Wash: mattwashauthor@gmail.com

www.jennyfordauthor.com

Acknowledgements

A big thank you to my ex-husband, Greg, for sharing his memories of our little one. He has helped remind me of things that, through grief, I had sub-consciously blanked out. Greg was incredible at keeping me strong whilst also trying to grieve himself. For that, I will forever be grateful.

To my beautiful children Sophie, Christian and Lucy… always know that your big sister is watching down on you.

Thank you to family and friends for their love and support through those very difficult times.

And finally, to you, the reader. I am so truly grateful that you have taken the time to share in my story.

Love and blessings.

About the author

Award Winning Inspirational Author Jenny Ford didn't set out to be a writer; in fact, no one was more surprised than Jenny when she wrote her first book. She was no A* student, and her lack of education was certainly not an indication that she would ever become an author.

Beauty was her first love but, when diagnosed with Multiple Sclerosis in 2010, she had to give up her highly successful mobile beauty therapist business for health and safety reasons. However, where many people may have struggled to emerge so positively from such a life change, Jenny soon discovered (thanks to a little Divine Intervention) that her true-life purpose was to write.

Jenny says. "I believe that my MS was a gift so that I could inspire and give hope to others. I fully believe that no matter what challenges we go through, there is always a way forward, a new path ahead and a more exciting journey to explore."

"Through my own adversity, I have learned to not only believe in myself but to accept my MS. My books bring positivity, healing and comfort to others through inspirational, heartfelt messages."

Reviews

"I was very privileged to read Jenny Ford's book 'The Loss of a Child'.

"The emotion that I felt was unbelievable, I cried like a baby! The sensitive subject that has been written with pure love, respect and raw emotion. I felt every single piece of hurt, love and grief written with every word. I highly recommend this amazing book but make sure you have tissues at the ready! This book gives you hope even after such a tragic loss. The writer definitely made me feel like I was there with her sharing in her love, pain and frustration. A beautifully written book and thank you for sharing your story."

~ Angie Johnstone Candler

"The loss of a child is utterly incomprehensible and is the hardest of losses to bear. While we feel Jenny's pain

and grief, we also experience with her, the healing that has taken place over the years.

"I know that by sharing her story, there will be many others who will find comfort in Jenny's writing."

~ **Melanie Moore**

"I can't recall ever reading a book that has tugged on my heart strings as much as this. A beautifully raw recount of how Jenny and Greg went through and came out the other side of, without question, the most devastating pain a person can face. As a father myself, I found this book inspiring and ever so moving. The human spirit should never be underestimated. Amazing effort, Jenny Ford. Highly recommended."

~ **Matt Wash**

"Very thoughtfully written. Child loss is such a difficult and emotive topic to write about.

"I really admire how Jenny thanked her ex-husband for keeping her strong. It's a real act of kindness to show

gratitude towards an ex-partner whilst reflecting on such a tragic time in your life.

"'The Loss of a Child' is a short story so as much as it's hard to read at times; particularly if you relate to the circumstances, it is manageable to digest.

"Catriona was born in 1991 and died seven-and-a-half months later.

"This is the devastating story of a mother's loss and her experience with the medical professionals and then sadly the Police after her daughters sudden death.

"Jenny's honesty shines through her writing and she even shares how the loss of Catriona ultimately affected her marriage.

"It's not a light read and it's quite dark at times but Jenny's writes with such tenderness and attention to small details that you will want to keep reading."

~ Eileen Morrison

In Loving Memory of our beautiful little angel, Catriona

1991-1992

Dedicated to all the parents who have lost a child.

And the family and friends also effected by the loss.

Jenny's Story

The loss of a child is unquestionably the hardest thing that a parent can go through; I know – I am one of those parents! No matter your child's age, and whether they die through illness (physically or mentally), natural causes, somebody else taking their life, miscarriage or still born–you just can't describe the harrowing emptiness you feel.

We lost our little girl, Catriona, in May 1992 when she was just seven-and-a-half months old. She was our first born; it took three years (with a little intervention) to conceive, and I remember so clearly the day I found out I was pregnant. It was the happiest day of our lives! I had a lovely pregnancy; everything was wonderful. On the 12th October, 1991, our little bundle of joy came into the world weighing 6lb 12oz; she had the most beautiful mop of dark hair. We finally had the child we so longed for. I remember that when Catriona was born, the midwife was slightly concerned.

"Something Wasn't

Quite Right"

She felt something wasn't quite right but couldn't explain what, so she asked the paediatrician to take a look at her. He said she was fine.

Catriona was a very happy baby - always giggling and smiling. She was very much a daddy's girl. Her eyes would light up every time he walked into the room. She loved playtime with him, and he spent every possible moment that he could with her. Greg would always sing to her, and those beautiful little eyes would gaze lovingly up at him. Every day was a blessing spent with our tiny one; little did we know what was to come.

One day, Catriona became very unsettled and refused to eat. Then over the next few days, she just constantly cried; it was heart-breaking. We checked everything we could think of but didn't know why she was so distressed. Greg held and soothed her for as long as it

took, and she appeared to recover. However, before long, she went back to crying inconsolably for hours on end. By this point we were very concerned, as this was not like her at all. Catriona was admitted to hospital for a week for tests. I stayed overnight with her, and Greg would visit every day. The doctors and nurses observed her but eventually concluded that it must be a virus. Despite the fact that she was still crying just as much as when she was admitted, they discharged her.

She did eventually settle, but I don't think she ever quite recovered from that virus. When I look back now, I can see that from the time she left the hospital, she didn't make much progress at all - and virtually stopped developing physically. Her weight levelled out, but she didn't show any symptoms of being ill - other than being prone to crying, which was very much out of character for her. The doctors and consultants assured us that she was just a small baby, but they intended to make further tests at some time in the future - just to be sure.

The health visitors would arrive and try different ways of feeding her, but Catriona just wasn't interested; this continued for quite a few months. We agonised over what our little girl was going through, that nobody could see. Was the midwife right to be concerned when Catriona was born? As first-time parents, you naturally follow the advice of the doctors and health visitors. We put our trust in them and did just that - which was to continue with what we were doing.

Catriona then developed a nasty little cold and cough, so we called the doctors' surgery. We were shocked to be told by the receptionist that there wasn't a free appointment for a week. Four days later, Greg was taking Catriona to church with him (as he did every Sunday), and I was going out with my friend Claire to buy Catriona a new buggy.

"Catriona Started

To Scream"

The one we had was kindly given to us by a friend, but it was starting to get a bit old and worn. It was a really hot day, so as I left the house, I told Greg to give Catriona a drink. After church, Greg took Catriona over to my friend Claire's house to have a little jamming session with her husband, Nigel. Both Greg and Nigel were very musical, and Catriona always loved hearing her daddy sing. Shortly after they arrived, Catriona started to scream. Greg tried to comfort her, but she just continued screaming hysterically; he then decided to take her back home.

After a little while, her screaming had turned into a whimper, and she just kept falling in and out of sleep. By this time, Greg was getting really concerned, so he called the out-of-hours'service; they told him that a doctor was on the way. Greg took Catriona's t-shirt off in case she was feeling too hot; by now, her breath had turned into a sigh, and she wasn't responding to him. He became increasingly anxious, as her limp little body lay sunk in his arms. When I arrived at our house, I began searching for my front door key. It was then I first heard Greg's voice through the window. He was repeatedly saying, "Come on, darling." As I

10

entered the house, he was just stood there holding our child, tears streaming down his face. There was clearly something seriously wrong with her –Catriona's breathing was very shallow, and I froze for a second - not quite taking in what he was saying. Then it hit me; instantly, I was hysterically sobbing and screaming, "Save her! Please save my baby!"

The ambulance arrived and put an oxygen mask on Catriona's tiny face. Greg asked if she was going to be okay, but they just replied that she was 'very poorly'. I remember quite clearly that my husband wasn't allowed to travel with her - which I couldn't understand. Only I was permitted to go in the ambulance, so a neighbour had to drive Greg to the hospital.

When the doctors returned from treating Catriona, Greg only had to see their faces to know what they

11

were about to tell him. As they looked darkly at eachother, one looked up and softly said, "We tried everything we could to save her –I'm so sorry." Everyone - even the nurses, were immediately in tears. Everyone except me that is; I refused to believe them, "It's not true – she's only asleep, isn't she?"

They brought Catriona in and gave her to Greg. He wept bitterly, as he lovingly cradled and kissed her. Tears rolled down his grief-stricken face, and loud sobs shook him uncontrollably. After a short while, I took my baby girl and sang one of her favourite songs, 'Old McDonald had a Farm', urging her to wake up for her lunch. But of course, she never did. For that brief moment, I had managed to shut out the reality of what had happened.

The most precious gift we could ever have wished for had been taken from us. It felt as though our very hearts had been ripped out.

That day will forever remain as the very worst of our lives.

"*The Very Worst Day*

Of Our Lives"

Because Catriona's passing was a sudden death, the police had to be informed. They were so cold towards us. Greg had to hand our baby's little body over to them so that she could be examined for any inflicted injuries. Greg then had to identify her for the purpose of the death certificate. That's when it really hit me. Greg also had to accompany the police back to the house so that they could examine the scene of the death. They even took the little t-shirt that she had been wearing, her blanket and her car seat -to search for any traces of blood. When they were satisfied that there was no foul play involved, the police softened their approach and became sympathetic and apologetic. They explained that, in their job, they had dealt with so many situations where parents had harmed and taken their children's lives that they couldn't treat us any differently. The officers then hugged us and left. They knew it was time for us to be with family and friends. Not only was losing our little

girl the worst possible thing to happen, but for people to think that we may have harmed her was just soul-destroying.

As it was a Bank Holiday, the post-mortem could not be carried out for several days. They kept her tiny body cool in the chapel of rest at the hospital, and we went to see her every day. The moment finally came when we were informed that the post-mortem had been completed, so we were free to lay our beautiful, little girl to rest.

The results of her death came back as Bronchial Phenomena. We couldn't believe that a slight cold and cough had turned into this; was it the result of the virus that she had a few months before? We went to see a specialist at the hospital, and she told us that there was nothing that we could have done to save Catriona – the illness just very quickly overwhelmed her. However, it could have been identified and dealt with if we had seen our GP when she first got it. We were angry - very angry; she was a fragile, poorly baby, and she should have had priority for a doctor's appointment. When we saw our GP, he was obviously

very apologetic - but it wasn't going to bring our little girl back. From that day on, things changed significantly at the surgery— every baby was a priority. To know that it took our daughter's death for that to happen is still so heart-breaking.

It was the day of Catriona's funeral, and the church was packed solid. There were no seats free or standing space left when our little girl was led down the aisle - carried by her besotted daddy. It was so tragic and distressing seeing Greg carry his little girl for the last time. I'll never forget the intermittent sounds of our loved-ones weeping. Catriona was so adored — not just by us, but the whole congregation. We then finished the service at her final resting place to say our goodbyes. It was the most distressing goodbye you could ever imagine. We visited Catriona's grave every single day for a year, and it was during that time that I found out I was pregnant again. After discovering that

"*Catriona Was*

So Adored"

we had fallen so quickly, it was an incredible feeling to know that we had been truly blessed once more.

The devastating recession of the 1990's arrived and Greg's work was badly hit; he had no choice but to accept some work in Paris for a year just so that we could keep our home. We rented the house out and, once it was safe for me to fly, I joined him. It was a stressful time being in a strange country, away from family and friends. I couldn't speak the language, with the little French that I did know being, "Une baguette, s'ilvous plait?" (One baguette please). Unsurprisingly, that didn't really get me very far with the locals! Thankfully, Greg did speak the language. In March, 1993, I gave birth to another beautiful little girl that we named Sophie. Amongst the initial joy, there was also a very scary moment. When Sophie was born, the nurse picked her up by the blanket she was wrapped in instead of (as you would do) by her body. Well, my heart sank as Sophie slipped out of her blanket heading for the cold hospital floor. I vividly remember pleading, "No, God – please, not again; I can't lose another child." Thankfully, and not for the first time, Greg was our guardian angel. He instinctively reached

out and caught our precious little one; he literally saved her life. I believe that Catriona was watching down on us at that moment and helped Greg to catch her little sister. The nurse just laughed as if it were an everyday occurrence. I wanted to swing for her, but luckily (for the nurse), I just couldn't move. I then so desperately wanted to get back home to England.

Two years later, our gorgeous little boy, Christian, was born. We had two healthy children, but any sign of the slightest sniffle, and I was down that doctors' surgery as a priority! Our family was complete - including our little angel in heaven who was watching down on us. When I look at Sophie and Christian now, I always wonder how much Catriona would have looked like them. You'd honestly think Sophie and Christian were twins - they look so alike!

Sadly, things took their toll on our marriage, and we later divorced. We both eventually remarried, and I had another beautiful daughter, Lucy.

It's been twenty-eight years since my little girl's passing and I'm fully aware that I (naturally) became very over-protective of my children – in fact, I still am!

But it has only been since writing this book that I have realised why. Besides the obvious reasons that I've shared with you here, it's largely because of the fact that I haven't totally healed - even after all this time.

After being interviewed about my other books, accepting and dealing with my health challenges (I have Multiple Sclerosis) and talking about the loss of my little girl to a friend, Melanie Moore, on her show Big Vision TV, the inspiration finally came to tell my story in written form. But why now – after all this time? I truly believe that I was guided by my little Catriona so that this book can help other parents that (at some time in their lives) have lost a child.

I feel that sharing and talking about the experience of child loss will not only help heal my own heart, but it will also help to heal others. We are not alone; we can understand that sadness, that pain, that broken heart,

"We Are

Not Alone"

that feeling of not being able to cope day after day. We have all been there- or are still going through it. Our departed, beautiful children were, and are, very much part of our lives. Whether they were with you for just a few minutes or for many years, I believe we should openly talk about them and celebrate the moments we had with them. It will undoubtedly be very difficult, and it may bring back memories that initially we don't want to face, but I'm certain that others could gain huge strength from our stories.

Your story, your strength and your support can help to heal in more ways than you could ever imagine. If you feel that talking is too hard, then try writing it down. As an author, I know how much healing the written word can provide. We all have our own story that affects us in different ways, but we do have that one thing in common that binds us together. It doesn't matter that we don't know each other, because the love we have for our little angels in heaven will always be there.

Thank you, Catriona, for showing me a love that I had never experienced before.

27

I Love You,

My Angel -

Always and

Forever.

Even though you are no longer here

Not a day goes by that I don't feel you near

My heart was crushed the day that you died

Putting back the pieces is hard, I can't deny

Each day I grow stronger, though painful as it is

I know for certain that would be your wish

I know you are safe, in the hands of the Lord

I pray that you know you were truly adored.

But know this, my precious, beautiful child…

Even though you seem so far away

You're always in my heart, each and every day.

After the Storm

For the first few months (after Catriona passed away), we were constantly surrounded by family and friends. This was of great comfort to us because having them around gave us something else to focus on. We were both extremely grateful for their love and support but, inevitably, the time came for them all to get back to their own lives - and that's when it really hit us.

Suddenly, it was now just the two of us in the house. Greg had to get back to work, and I would just walk around the house, not really knowing what to do with myself. Day after day, I would just sit holding on to Catriona's little toys, smelling her clothes - being crushed by the realisation that she was actually gone. I remember just crying for hours on end, unable to stop myself. Poor Greg really struggled, too, but he had to carry on working so we could keep the roof over our heads. He found that ever so tough.

Back then, we were never really given any support other than from our family and friends. No organisation was available back then to help us deal with the grief, so we were pretty much left to do the best we could by ourselves. The experience we had following Catriona's passing played a huge role in me becoming involved with the charity 'Child Bereavement UK'. No parent should be expected to overcome such a massive loss without the support of these valuable, specialist groups.

At the time, I also found it difficult when I was out, especially as I'd see people that I had known for years actually cross to the other side of the road because they felt uncomfortable and awkward. I would get annoyed and upset but, on reflection, I fully understand now why people would find it difficult to know what to say. It really was a horrible time for everyone involved.

We all have our own way of dealing with grief; there's no right way or wrong way - only your way! However, I do feel strongly that everyone deserves the right to

have a support group that they can turn to during those incredibly painful times.

Sending love and blessings to each and every mum, dad, brother, sister, grandparent, niece, nephew, uncle and auntie who has ever lost a precious loved one.

Precious Memories

. . . .

. . . .

. . . .

. . . .

. . . .

. . . .

. . . .

. . . .

. . . .

. . . .

. . . .

. . . .

. . . .

. . . .

. . . .

. . . .

. . . .

. . . .

. . . .

. . . .

. . . .

. . . .

. . . .

. . . .

. . . .

. . . .

. . . .

. . . .

. . . .

. . . .

. . . .

. . . .

. . . .

. . . .

. . . .

. . . .

. . . .

. . . .

. . . .

. . . .

. . . .

Grief Support

If you've experienced the loss of a child there are many organisations that can help. Including **Child Bereavement UK**, who support families and educate professionals when a baby or child of any age dies or is dying, or when a child is facing bereavement.

Get in contact at:
Helpline: 0800 02 888 40
support@childbereavementuk.org
www.childbereavementuk.org

Other books that can help cope with the loss of a loved one include:

The Grief Garden Path by Julie New
www.theendlessbookcase.com/e-books/the-grief-garden-path/

Sibling Bereavement by Ann Farrant
www.theendlessbookcase.com/e-books/sibling-bereavement/

Also by Jenny Ford

A Collection of Inspirational Guided Prayers

A collection of 40 short prayers covering a range of subjects, solely to bring a sense of peace and comfort.

Messages to Inspire Your Day

Intuitively written messages to bring a sense of peace, love and joy. They can be used for daily guidance or whenever you feel the need for some inspiration to help you walk the path of life.

Whether the message is for yourself or for you to bring a piece of love and comfort to someone else, know that divine guidance from God and the angels will be with you.

Cards for Guidance

Cards for Guidance have the same messages as in 'Messages to Inspire your Day', except in card form. There are 25 vibrantly coloured cards in the deck, each one with its own inspiring message. They come in a handmade, purple velvet pouch with a crystal gem bead and charm placed around the neck of the pouch.

These cards can only be purchased through my online shop at: www.jennyfordauthor.com.

Prisoner Within

Reeling in heartache and pain, Amy is trapped in a world of nightmares, becoming a prisoner in her own mind and finding it difficult to let go and forgive.

This is Amy's journey to finding inner peace!

Gabriella's Travels

The plane lands. With excitement and anticipation, Gabriella steps onto British soil, the first destination of her journey. Never having left her home town in Positano, Southern Italy before, she had always dreamt of this moment.

What was in store for Gabriella on this amazing adventure?

Tilly and the Magical Mermaid

Tilly is at her happiest when she is at the beach looking for different kinds of shells and pebbles. She also has a great imagination, as she discovers whilst out fishing with her Grandpa. But is it her imagination or is it real?

This story colouring book is educational, engaging and fun. It has been created to capture the imagination of all young readers. They are encouraged to write their own story by using the blank and lined pages at the back of this book, whether it be with words or pictures, to bring out their creativity. For ages 5-8.

Joshua and the Magical Unicorn

Joshua just loves unicorns! He has unicorn books, unicorn toys, unicorn ornaments; he even dreams of unicorns! Then one day, as Joshua is reading one of his books, he drifts off into a daydream. What happens next surprises Joshua.

This story colouring book is educational, engaging and fun. It has been created to capture the imagination of all young readers. They are encouraged to write their own story by using the blank and lined pages at the back of this book, whether it be with words or pictures, to bring out their creativity. For ages 5-8.

BV - #0042 - 040520 - C0 - 170/140/4 - PB - 9781912243976